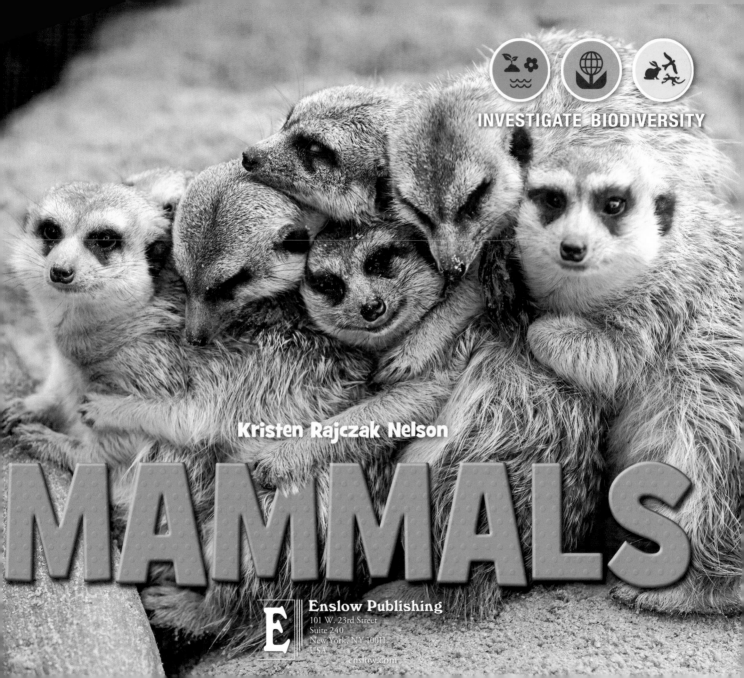

INVESTIGATE BIODIVERSITY

Kristen Rajczak Nelson

MAMMALS

Enslow Publishing
101 W. 23rd Street
Suite 240
New York, NY 10011
USA
enslow.com

●●● Words to Know

adapt To change.

climate The average weather of a place.

developed To be more grown.

ecosystem Everything that lives in an area.

habitat The place where an animal lives.

predator An animal that hunts another animal.

prey An animal that is hunted by another animal.

protect To keep safe.

species A group of living things that are similar.

survive To continue to live.

temperature How hot or cold something is.

variety A number of different things.

Contents

Magnificent Mammals

There are more than 5,000 **species**, or kinds, of mammals on Earth. There are lots of different kinds of mammals. But all mammals have certain things in common.

What Makes a Mammal?

Mammals all have a backbone. They breathe air. They are all warm-blooded. This means that their bodies stay at a constant **temperature** no matter how hot or cold it is around them. All mammals have hair or fur at some point in their life. But the most important thing about mammals? Mammal mothers grow babies inside their bodies. Most give birth to live young. Mammal mothers make milk in their bodies for their babies to drink.

Humans and their pet dogs have at least one thing in common: they're all mammals!

It Takes All Kinds

Mammals do have lots of similarities. But the mammal group is also full of **variety**! Mammals can be different sizes, shapes, and colors. Some, like the blue whale, are huge. Blue whales can be up to 100 feet (30.5 meters) long! Other mammals are very small. The bumblebee bat only

Dolphins are one kind of mammal that lives in the sea. Some others are seals, whales, and manatees.

Fast Fact

There are more than seven billion of one kind of mammal on Earth: people!

weighs about 0.07 ounce (2 grams)! Mammals such as dogs, cats, and horses are almost totally covered in fur. Whales, though, only have some hair when they are still growing inside their mother.

All of these body differences make mammals a fascinating animal group. And it's extra special because we're part of it!

Adapting and Surviving

● ● ● Mammals live in many kinds of **habitats**. They can be found in rain forests or on mountains. They can live in the desert or in the ocean. We already learned that mammals are warm-blooded animals. This means that they can live in tropical **climates** where it's hot and wet most of the year. They can also be found in very cold parts of Earth. Polar bears are mammals that live in northern Canada and Russia. Animals have **adapted** to help their species **survive** wherever they live. Polar bears have a layer of fat on their body that keeps them warm and helps them swim.

Swinging and Swimming

Mammals' bodies have adapted according to how they live and move. Monkeys often live among trees. They can swing from branch to branch with long

The arctic fox has adapted to its cold habitat. It has fur on the soles of its feet and its white coat blends in with the snow.

arms and feet that look like a person's hand. Dolphins use fins to swim through the water. Wolves can run fast on four legs to hunt and get where they're going.

Safety and Survival

All mammals have adaptations that help them find food and stay safe. Black panthers have black fur and hunt at night so they can't be seen. They also have big, sharp teeth. Those teeth come in handy when they are hunting. Some kinds of rabbits change color as the seasons change. They turn from brown to white when winter comes to blend in

Fast Fact

Adaptations are changes to an animal's body or how the animal acts. These changes take place over a long time. They help a species live in their habitat better.

Howler monkeys live in the tropical forests of Central and South America. They have a tail that acts like an extra arm. It helps them hang from branches.

with the snow. This adaptation is called camouflage. These and more adaptations help mammals survive in their habitat.

Social Lives of Mammals

The way a mammal lives affects its chances of surviving. Lions, elephants, and chimpanzees are all mammals that live and work together. Often, these groups help raise young. Animals may have special jobs, too. In a pride of lions, the male lions **protect** their group. Female lions take care of the young and hunt.

Meerkats live in large groups. They help each other build their homes and take care of their young.

Other mammals live alone. Moose, bears, and skunks are all mammals that spend most of their time alone. Often this is because it is easier for them to find food on their own.

The Circle of Life

The life cycle of all mammals starts the same way. The female finds a male mate. Then, the female carries the young as it grows in her body. Some mammals, such as humans, usually have one baby at a time. Other mammals may have six or more young at once!

How long a mammal carries her young depends on the species. Elephant babies grow inside their mothers for almost two years. Tiger mothers only carry their babies

Fast Fact

Mammals have different ways of getting a mate. Some males fight each other for females!

Baby elephants are called calves. They stay close to their mothers for several years.

for about three and a half months. The usual time for humans is nine months.

Marsupials are one group of mammals that carry their babies for a very short time. The young of kangaroos, koalas, and opossums are born before they are fully **developed**. They are born and then crawl right into their mother's pouch. There, they drink her milk and grow more.

Special Mammals

There is one small group of mammals that start life a bit differently. These mammals are called monotremes. They are unique because they lay eggs. Platypuses and echidnas are part of this group. They only live in Australia, Tasmania, and New Guinea. Even though

Baby echidnas hatch from eggs. They are part of the monotreme group of mammals.

A baby koala is a joey. It spends its first six months in its mother's pouch. Then it climbs onto her back for a ride.

they don't have live babies, monotremes do make milk for their young to drink.

Mother and Child

Once mammal babies are born, their mother usually cares for them. She may have help from other members of the animal group. These adult mammals show the young mammals how to find food. They also teach them to hide from **predators**. Koala babies stay with their mother for a long time. They ride on her back, often until she has another baby!

Once a mammal becomes an adult, the life cycle begins again. How long it takes to become an adult depends on the species.

Mammals and the Food Chain

Mammals have lots of different eating habits. Mammals such as cows, hippos, and koalas are herbivores. This means they only eat plant material such as grass, leaves, and roots. Carnivores are animals that only eat other animals. Lions and wolves are carnivores. Omnivores like bears, raccoons, and pigs eat both plants and animals!

Mammal versus Mammal

Mammals play an important role in the many **ecosystems** in which they live. They're a very important part of the food chain. In the food chain, energy is passed from one living thing to another in the form of food. A rabbit may eat grass. Then a fox eats the rabbit. Each living thing gets energy from what it eats.

Many mammals are predators. They might find other mammals to eat, such as the zebras that lions hunt. So,

A giant panda munches on some bamboo.

mammals can be both the hunter and the food! Both are important. Without the predator, too many of the **prey** mammal might survive. Without the prey, the predator species might go hungry and die out.

Links in the Food Chain

Mammals do not only affect the other animals in the food chain. They can also have an important effect on plants. Many mammals eat parts of plants. They help spread the seeds in their waste. Some kinds of bats

Fast Fact

A food chain is the way scientists show how living things depend on each other as a source of food.

A long-nosed bat eats an agave flower.

20

A cheetah races after a springbok in Africa. If it catches it, the springbok will be the cheetah's next meal.

drink the sweet matter plants make, called nectar. While the bat drinks, pollen from the plants sticks to it. When the bat flies to another flower, it carries the pollen, too! This helps plants continue to grow.

All of the food chains connect in a bigger food web of an ecosystem—and mammals are a main part of it! They're an interesting and important part of our world.

Activity: Healthy Habitats

● ● ● 1. Using a book or the internet, look up the different habitats where mammals may live. Choose one that interests you.

2. Find out what kinds of food chains mammals in that habitat are part of. Write them out on a piece of paper.

3. Cross out one mammal in the food chain. What would happen if that mammal died out and was no longer part of the food chain?

4. Choose another mammal to cross out. What happens to the food chain and ecosystem now?

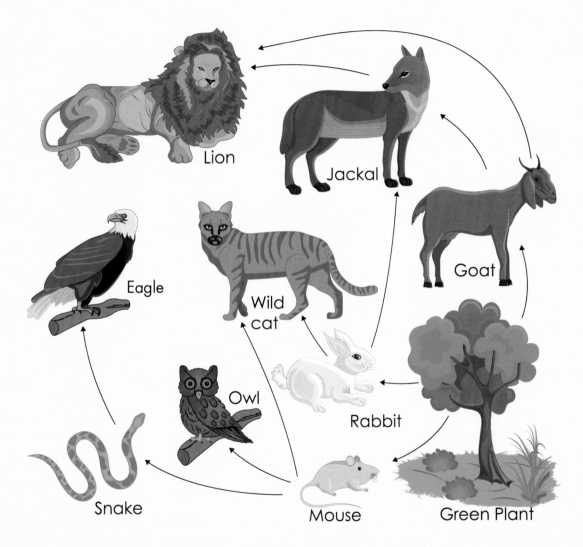

Lion

Jackal

Goat

Eagle

Wild cat

Owl

Rabbit

Snake

Mouse

Green Plant

All of the animals in the food chain get energy from other plants and animals. The sun and water give plants energy.

Learn More

Books

Howell, Izzi. *Mammals*. New York, NY: Windmill Books, 2018.

Jacobson, Bray. *Mammal Life Cycles*. New York, NY: Gareth Stevens Publishing, 2018.

Royston, Angela. *Mammals*. Chicago, IL: Heinemann, 2015.

Websites

National Geographic Kids: Mammals
kids.nationalgeographic.com/animals/hubs/mammals
Check out all kinds of cool mammals on this website.

San Diego Zoo Kids: Animals
adminkids.sandiegozoo.org/animals
Get facts and photos about your favorite mammal.

Index

Published in 2019 by Enslow Publishing, LLC.
101 W. 23rd Street, Suite 240, New York, NY 10011

Copyright © 2019 by Enslow Publishing, LLC.

Library of Congress Cataloging-in-Publication Data
Names: Rajczak Nelson, Kristen, author.
Title: Mammals / Kristen Rajczak Nelson.
Description: New York : Enslow Publishing, 2019. | Series: Investigate biodiversity | Audience: Grade K-4. | Includes bibliographical references and index.
Identifiers: LCCN 2018004943| ISBN 9781978501959 (library bound) | ISBN 9781978502505 (paperback) | ISBN 9781978502512 (6 pack)
Subjects: LCSH: Mammals—Juvenile literature.
Classification: LCC QL706.2 .R35 2019 | DDC 599—dc23
LC record available at https://lccn.loc.gov/2018004943

Printed in the United States of America

To Our Readers: We have done our best to make sure all website addresses in this book were active and appropriate when we went to press. However, the author and the publisher have no control over and assume no liability for the material available on those websites or on any websites they may link to. Any comments or suggestions can be sent by email to customerservice@enslow.com.

Photos Credits: Cover, p. 1 nattanan726/Shutterstock.com; pp. 3, 14 Albie Venter/Shutterstock.com; pp. 3, 15 Roland Seitre/Minden Pictures/Getty Images; pp. 3, 9 outdoorsman/Shutterstock.com; pp. 3, 11 JPL Designs/Shutterstock.com; pp. 3, 5 Pressmaster/Shutterstock.com; p. 6 Andrea Izzotti/Shutterstock.com; p. 12 Raju Soni/Shutterstock.com; p. 16 Alizada Studios/Shutterstock.com; p. 18 Photo By Lola/Shutterstock.com; p. 20 Danita Delmont/Shutterstock.com; p. 21 Elana Erasmus/Shutterstock.com; p. 23 snapgalleria/Shutterstock.com; cover graphics magic pictures/Shutterstock.com.